I LOVE MYTHOLOGY

The Olympians

Texts: Anastasia D. Makri

Illustrator: Iulios Maroulakis

Translated from Greek into English

Kiriaki Papakonstantinou

BA English Language & Literature / MA Psycholinguistics / DIPTRANS - DPSI
Chartered Linguist (Translator) / Translators - Interpreters Trainer
Member of the Chartered Institute of Linguists in London

UNDER THE AEGIS OF

UNESCO
United Nations
Educational, Scientific
& Cultural Organization

ΟΜΙΛΟΣ ΓΙΑ ΤΗΝ UNESCO ΝΟΜΟΥ ΠΕΙΡΑΙΩΣ & ΝΗΣΩΝ
CLUB FOR UNESCO OF THE DEPARTMENT OF PIRAEUS & ISLANDS
Πέτρου Ράλλη 210 & Θησέως 1 Νίκαια,
Τηλ.: 210 4967757, Fax: 210 4944564 - www.unescopireas.gr e-mail: unescop@otenet.gr

AGYRA
publications

The life of the gods
on Mount Olympus

Ancient Greeks believed that gods lived in a shining palace on top of Mount Olympus, the highest mountain in Greece, where they observed people from. The Olympians were enormous in size and more beautiful than humans.

Ancient Greeks believed their gods were almighty, immortal and could do miracles, they lived in joy, eating

ambrosia – the divine food – and drinking nectar, the wine of the gods. But just like humans, gods had their strengths and weaknesses as well. They loved, hated, and fell passionately in love! They would stand by people, but when they were angry with humans, they punished them harshly.

The Olympians were twelve, however, there were also lesser gods called demigods.

Zeus (Jupiter)

Zeus was King of humans and gods. He controlled the lives and fate of humans and held the thunder in his hands; for this reason he was called Thunder-Striker. He was also called Cloud-Gatherer because he stirred up the clouds and caused rain to fall upon the earth. People imagined him sitting on a throne made of gold and ivory, with a thunderbolt in one hand and his scepter in the other. Zeus had two jars containing good things and bad things which he dispensed to mortals, depending on their behavior. However, both gods and humans feared his rule. Zeus was also the god of hospitality.

Hera

Hera was the wife of Zeus and Queen of the Olympians. She was beautiful and majestic, sitting on her throne next to Zeus, crowned with sunbeams. She was holding a pomegranate in her hand and had peacocks at her feet, symbols of her pride and beauty.

Hera was the most respected of all goddesses and people used to build altars and temples in her honor. Her favorite city, Argos, honored her most. But when Zeus, her husband, loved other women, so much was her rage that she had an urge to avenge.

Athena

Athena, the favorite daughter of Zeus, was born fully armed from his forehead. And that's how the story goes.

Zeus mated with beautiful and wise Metis. Yet, there was an oracle[1] saying that Metis would give birth first to a daughter and then to a son, who would become ruler of gods and humans. On hearing such an oracle, Zeus got anxious and rushed to ask the advice of Gaia and Uranus, on what to do. "Swallow your pregnant wife before she gives birth to your child" was their advice. Zeus immediately followed their words and swallowed his pregnant wife. But when the time had come the pains of childbirth were driving Zeus crazy. He immediately called for his son Hephaestus and asked him to open up his head with an ax. So, the goddess of wisdom, Athena sprang fully armed, with helmet and spear.

---

1. **Oracle:** the place where people communicated with gods seeking for advice as well as the answer/advice given by the priest or priestess to people concerning their future.

Athena was the patron goddess of Athens, which was named after her. She offered Athenians the olive tree, which is the symbol of peace and they built the Parthenon and celebrated the Panathenean festival in her honor.

Poseidon (Neptune)

Poseidon was the god of the sea, earthquakes and horses and second in power after his brother Zeus. He lived less on Mount Olympus and more into the sea depths. With his trident in hand and a herd of dolphins following him, he loved wandering around the sea. When he was angry, he struck the water with his trident and a giant tidal wave would come rushing. Poseidon was also called Earth-Shaker because when the he stirred up the sea with his formidable trident, the earth trembled and shook. His wife was Amphitrite, the daughter of Oceanus. Poseidon gave the horse to the humans, who honored him organizing horse races at the festivals called Poseidonia.

7

Demeter

Demeter was the goddess of earth, grain and fertility. She did not stay long on Olympus because when Pluto, the god of the Dead, fell in love with her daughter, the beautiful Persephone, Demeter wandered around Greece with a torch in hand, to find her. She reached the Palace of King Keleos at Eleusis. There, she was welcomed with great joy and the goddess, in order to repay their hospitality, taught them how to cultivate wheat and grains and how to tame wild animals. The people of Eleusis held the Thesmophoria festival and the Eleusinian mysteries in honor of her.

Demeter, desperate for not finding her daughter, threatened Zeus to barren the earth, so that people would die of hunger. Then

Zeus agreed with Pluto Persephone to stay in Hades for four months and with her mother for the rest eight months of the year.

Apollo

Apollo was god of the Sun, Prophecy and Music. He was the most beautiful son of Zeus and the mortal beauty Leto. He was also the twin brother of goddess Artemis.

When Hera found out about Leto, chased her and she fled to the island of Delos, where she gave birth to her twins. So, Delos became the sacred island of ancient Greeks. Apollo was also worshiped at Delphi, where there was the famous oracle. There, Pythia gave people the oracles informing them about the will of the gods.

Hermes (Mercury)

Hermes was the son of Zeus and Maia, daughter of Atlas. He was born in a cave on the Kyllini Mountain. From an early age his brilliance was evident. He was the messenger of the Olympians and the god of profit and commerce. He was called wing-legged because he was wearing winged sandals and cap, to fly swiftly.

When he was young, he created the first lyre from a tortoise shell. Later, he went to Pieria where he stole Apollo's cattle and brought them to Pylos. Zeus intervened to reconcile

the two brothers. All ended well. Hermes offered his lyre to Apollo, and Apollo let him keep his oxen.

Artemis

Artemis, the goddess of hunting, carried a bow and a quiver of arrows, but she was not involved in wars. She was a peaceful goddess, who loved animals and spent most of her time in the countryside, surrounded by the nymphs. The deer and the bear were her symbols. She also protected women who had difficult childbirth.

When she was a young girl, she told her father, Zeus, that she did not want to get marries, as she preferred to run free on the mountains and valleys.

Ares (Mars)

Ares was the god of war. He was the son of Zeus and Hera and always ready for war. The people dreaded him and they never honored him with sacrifices. Even his father, Zeus, was not much fond of him because he was always involved in quarrels and fights.

Eris was Ares' sister, who the god of war always took with him to sow discord. Ares fought with the Trojans against the Greeks. His wife was the most beautiful Aphrodite. She had chosen him as her husband instead of lame Hephaestus, whom she was forced to marry. The union of Ares and Aphrodite gave birth to Harmony.

Aphrodite (Venus)

Aphrodite was the most beautiful of all goddesses. She suddenly risen from the foam of the waves close to Cyprus; that's why she was also called Kyprogeneia.

She was the goddess of beauty, love and protector of the orphans and girls. Her first husband was unsightly Hephaestus, but later she married Ares, and they had a

13

beautiful baby boy, Eros. People loved her dearly and built beautiful temples in her honor.

Hephaestus

Hephaestus was the god of fire and blacksmiths, son of Zeus and Hera, who was so ugly by birth that his mother kicked him away only to land on the island of Lemnos. As he fell to the ground, he broke his leg and was lame. There, on Lemnos, he set up his smithery and manufactured ironware and weapons for the gods. Actually, he was the one who made the arms of Achilles.

Hestia

Goddess Hestia was respected and highly appreciated by ancient Greeks. In fact, her statue was put by the fireplace. She was the most modest of the single goddesses and the protector of home and family. She lived on Olympus guarding the palace of the gods. People first made their sacrifices to Hestia and then the other gods.

Pluto and Dionysus

We have seen the twelve Olympians, the twelve major gods. However, there was also the god of the underworld, Pluto or Hades, as well as Dionysus, son of Zeus and princess Semele. Merry Dionysus, wreathed in ivy and vine branches, was the god of grapes and wine. He liked to live near people and feast with his friends, the Nymphs.

Akis Melachris

Can you find out which is the shadow
of goddess Hestia?

Two out of the six details do not match the picture above.
Can you find which ones?

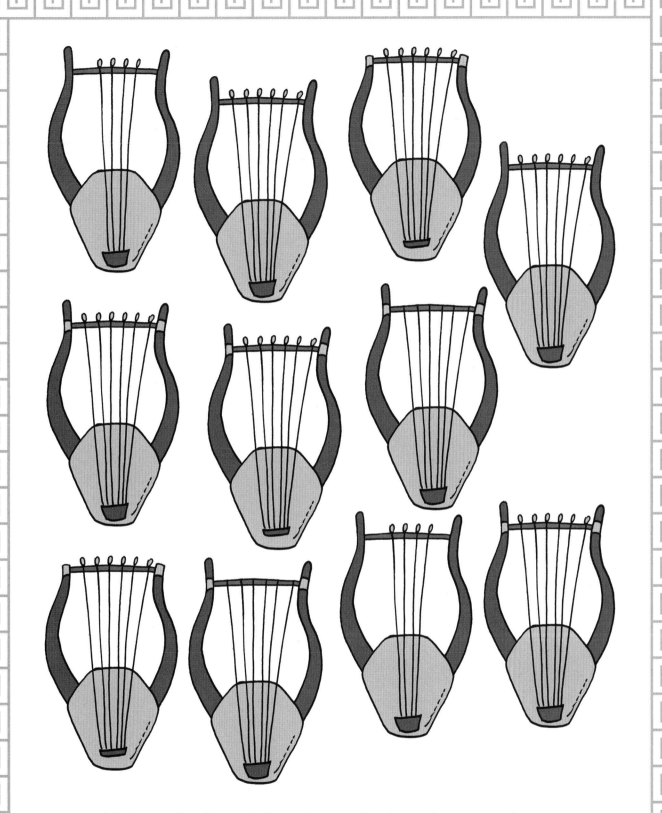

All lyres in the picture have their pair, except one.
Can you find it?

19

Connect the dots from 1 to 44,
to see what is sketched.

Put the letters in the correct order,
to see who the woman god Pluto loves is.

E	P	L	U	T	O	A	R	D	E	M	E	S	A
Q	O	E	M	E	A	T	I	I	R	A	L	H	M
I	S	A	B	A	P	H	R	O	D	I	T	E	P
H	E	R	A	W	H	E	U	N	J	M	A	R	J
A	I	T	C	R	Y	N	T	Y	O	R	I	M	O
K	D	E	H	E	Z	A	A	S	Y	O	Q	E	Y
U	O	M	O	F	O	R	I	U	A	R	E	S	Z
R	N	I	P	E	Z	E	U	S	L	E	W	H	E
O	I	S	E	W	H	D	E	M	E	T	E	R	L
S	C	O	R	Q	U	E	R	I	M	A	B	L	O
H	E	P	H	A	E	S	T	U	S	H	E	L	R

In the word-finding grid, horizontally and vertically, there are the names of 12 gods. Can you find them?

Can you find out which is the shadow
of goddess Athena?

Color the dot pieces to see
what the hidden picture is.

Which path should god Dionysus
take to get to the wine?

Which numbers correspond to goddess Artemis
and the deer, so as to verify the operations?

Connect the dots from 1 to 49,
to see what is sketched.

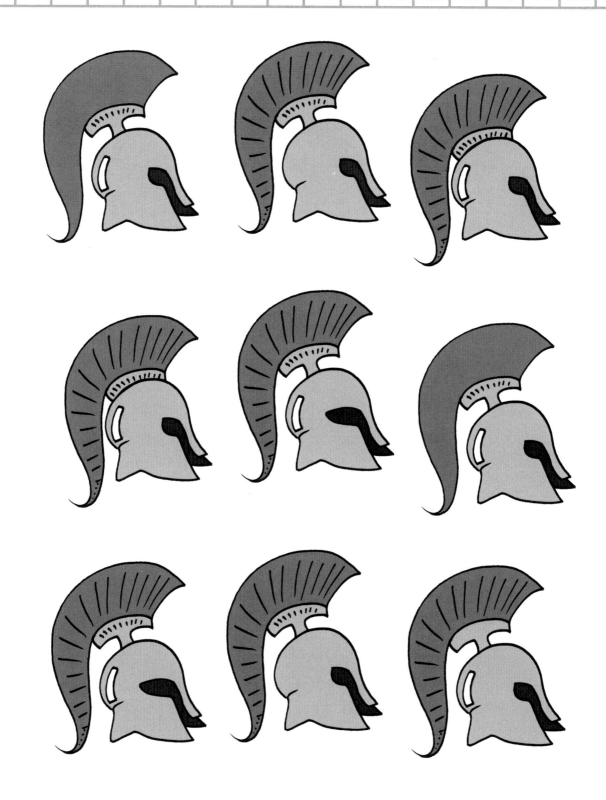

All helmets in the picture have their pair, except one.
Can you find it?

There are 4 errors in the picture.
Can you find them?

Spot-the-Difference: Can you find the 8 differences between image and its negative?

Spot-the-Difference: Pictures 2 and 3 have 3 differences each with Picture 1. Can you spot them?

SOLUTIONS

PAGE 17 Shadow No 2.

PAGE 18 Details No 1 and 6.

PAGE 19

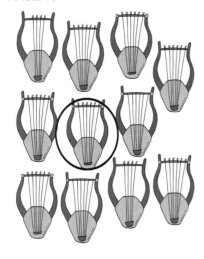

PAGE 21 Pluto loves PERSEPHONE.

PAGE 22

PAGE 23 Shadow No 3.

PAGE 24

PAGE 25 Path C.

PAGE 26 Artemis = 4 = 5 deer.

PAGE 28

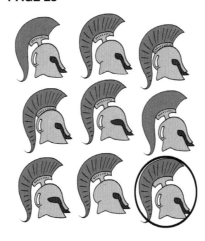

PAGE 29

PAGE 30

PAGE 31

Cover and interior design: Efthimis Dimoulas

© 2012 D.A. PAPADIMITRIOU S.A. «AGYRA» Publications
The present edition, May 2017
271 L. Katsoni str. • Ag. Anargiroi P.O. 135 62 Athens, Greece
Tel.: +30 210 2693800-4 - Fax: +30 210 2693806-7 • e-mail: info@e-agyra.gr • www.e-agyra.gr

ISBN: 978-960-547-007-4
Produced in Greece